Be Blessed

Udo Ufomadu

Be Blessed

Udo Ufomadu

© 2009 by Dr. Udo F. Ufomadu. All rights reserved.

Printed in the United States of America.

No part of this publication may be reproduced, stored in a retrieval system, or transmitted in a way by any means--electronic, mechanical, photocopy, recording, or otherwise--without the prior permission of the copyright holder, except as provided by USA copyright law.

Scripture references marked KJV are taken from the King James Version of the Bible.

Published by:

UFOMADU CONSULTING & PUBLISHING

P.O. Box 746

Selma, AL 36701

www.ufomaduconsulting.com

ISBN 978-0-9790022-2-9

Library of Congress Catalog Card Number: 2009904144

Contents

God's Child	17
Be Blessed	18
God is With You	19
Glorious	20
Divine Promise	21
Divine Relationship	22
Stupendous	23
No More	24
What's Love?	25
Dignity	26
It's Time Y'all	27
God's Encouragement	28
Genuine Factors	29
I Know Love	30
United We're Stronger	31
Significant 3:16	32
Love Defined	33
BOUNCING	34
WE GOT POWER	35
Ever Blessed	36
GOOD HUSTLIN'	37
God Bless You	38

Acknowledgments

To God be all glory and adoration forevermore.

Prologue

When God inspired some people to write for the Bible, He motivated them to write in prose and poetic forms. No wonder we have poetic expressions and figures of speech throughout the Bible, such as simile, metaphor, personification, and synonymous parallelism. Check out these superlative SIMILES: "But my horn You have exalted like a wild ox; I have been anointed with fresh oil....The righteous shall flourish like a palm tree, He shall grow like a cedar in Lebanon" (Psalm 92:10,12). "But the path of the just is like the shining sun" (Proverbs 4:18). To add, PERSONIFICATION is so effectively used in the Bible that it makes you want to read a verse over and over. In the Book of Proverbs, chapter 3 verses 15-18, "wisdom" is so amazingly personified that it gets the reader's attention as though wisdom is a person: "She is more precious than rubies, And all the things you may desire cannot compare with her. Length of days is in her right hand. In her left hand riches and honor. Her ways are ways of pleasantness, and all her paths are peace. She is a tree of life to those who take hold of her. And happy are all who retain her."

As a matter of certainty, the REPETITIVE/EMPHATIC poetic styles or use of SYNONYMOUS PARALLELISM styles by great poets are depicted throughout the Book of Psalm and Ecclesiastes. "Let Israel now say His mercy endures forever. Let the house of Aaron now say his mercy endures forever. Let those who fear the Lord now say His mercy endures forever" (Psalm 118:2-4).

In Ecclesiastes chapter 3, a reader is forced to grasp, through emphatic style, that there is a season, or time, for everything--a time to heal, a time to build up, a time to keep silent, a time to speak, a time to love, a time to dance, and etc. In SYNONYMOUS PARALLELISM, the second line is repeated in a different form but retains the meaning of the first line for emphasis.

The Book of Proverbs, the Book of Ecclesiastes, the Songs of Solomon, the Book of Isaiah, etc. are all true manifestations of commendable poetic works. Personally, I had thought that my book of poems/proses, *Anthology of Inspiration*, would be my last book of poems. However, I could not say no to God because He kept giving me poems to write.

Personally, I believe that God loves poetry because children, as well as adults, can identify with it. Poetry attracts the attention of all ages and all backgrounds. Enjoy this book, be blessed, and bless others with it. I definitely believe that when we genuinely immerse ourselves in the business of blessing and encouraging others, that's when blessings are overly drawn to us. When our prayer to God is not self-centered and goes beyond our immediate family, that's when we experience great success the "God's way".

We should endeavor to walk in unity and in love always. We cannot afford to hate others for their sacrifices in life, for what they have, for how they positively carry themselves, and for how they look. I strongly believe that the

"Blesser" is still in the business of blessing us if we are willing to sacrifice and obey according to a paramount scriptural philosophy, "Give, and it shall be given unto you" (Luke 6:38). So if a person gives hate, that person shall receive hate. If you give love and kindness, you shall receive love and kindness. If you give money for good reasons, you will not lack money. If you give quality time to your study/education, you'll receive quality grades and a quality career as God proposes.

God's Child

Nevertheless I know you are

A child of the Most High God

Not evaluating by your car

Not evaluating by your "bling-bling"

Not evaluating by your house

Not evaluating by your job title

Nevertheless I know you are

A child of the Most High God

The attacks are temporary

Not judging by them

The storm is temporary

Not judging by it

The warfare is temporary

Not judging by it

The fall is temporary

Not judging by it

All the same I know you are

A child of the Most High God

Your testimonies are fruits so beloved

Your praises to God are fruits so cherished

Your worship to God is a duty so prized

Your love for others is a fruit so treasured

Your presence is always a fruit so gorgeous

And by your fruits you've been known.

Be Blessed

They are incessant attacks because of what the enemies and head enemy know

Constant temptations are so as the devil and followers palpably see

On your life the favor of God manifesting

On your works the light of God radiating

Stand tall and audaciously praise Who clears your ways

Be ye therefore a follower and doer of what God clearly says

He will not fail you, you must believe

He poured His blessings, you must receive

Enjoy your blessings I said

Value up dearly the price He paid

Be encouraged for Jesus prayed for you

As the devil and "hate machines" cannot devour you

God is With You

What did you say?

Enjoy your blessings

Come again?

Value up the price Jesus paid

What now?

There is God's favor on your life

Pardon?

Stand tall and praise God audaciously

Could you repeat that?

He will not fail you

What?

He cares for you

You can say that again!

God loves you

I beg your pardon?

The devil and hate machines cannot devour you.

Glorious

Be reassured that fierce attacks precede glorious victories

As we wage wars against evil storms

But the tougher the wars, the more glorious the victories

Be strong, be tough, and be firm on your trust

Protect us Lord we pray

And tell us what to say

For when it storms this way

We pray for You to stay

As impious wind blows saints

Look Up and do not fret

For the triumph is so imminent

Oh yes, victory looming with intent.

Divine Promise

The declaration is extensive and infinite,

And He is realistic and just Who has guaranteed

To dispense water plentifully upon the thirsty

And floods upon dry ground

To bestow heavenly peace in us in excess

As our prayer line enjoys unlimited access

Because He overcame the world perfectly

To be our help all the time

And never leave nor forsake us

To freely give all things

And lavish love on the chosen

To give us a new heart

And put new spirit within us

Oh yes, the assertion is huge and immeasurable

And He is trustworthy and steadfast Who has promised

To unselfishly give us the kind of glory His father gave Him

That we may be one as He and His father are one

To send us an unchanging Comforter, an astute Consultant, a Prudent teacher

To teach us all things in diversified ways

To make us siblings if we receive Him

To give us wisdom if we ask the Generous Father

To overflow our harvest containers if we don't give up

To guide us along the best pathway for our life

To advise and watch over us

To heal the broken hearts

And utterly bind up their wounds.

Divine Relationship

More of your love

Dear Lord

More of Leadership

Heavenly Father

Our wings of praise will not tire

As we ascend gracefully higher

A lovely role that draws us to the Highest God

A positioning that lifts us to the Perfect Lord

More of Your influence

We legitimately long for

More of your Love

We candidly desire

Direct me straight to that well of peace

Quench my thirst from that fountain of higher love

Give me the daily wisdom from You

Show me how to walk at all times on the street of maximum faith

More of Your direction

Oh God

More of Your Spirit

Dear Lord.

Stupendous

Working hard to work against God's favor

Thou reapest no good in any way

Working hard to not work against goodness

Thou reapest well in every way

It was meant to be a blessing for all

But some recipients of the sacrifice

Maliciously turned them to coals of fire

On their heads

A pertinent choosing contest alright

Some choose friendship and alliance

Some choose enmity and antagonism

Some choose thoughtfulness and fairness

Some obeyed the MHG (Most High God)

Some obeyed the MHD (Most High deceiver)

Some received their blessings

Some received coals of fire on their heads

Without dissimulation

Without envy

Without anger

Some loved and shared

Devoid of restrictions

Devoid of reservations

Devoid of oppositions

Many were incalculably blessed.

No More

It is bleeding profusely

The hand cannot clasp

The hand is hurting

It is willing though

To make the mouth smile

But cannot hold on

Because it is still sore

It is still bleeding

From the bite

For the mouth has bitten

The finger that feeds her

It is about love

It is about genuine apology

It is about God in you

It is about regret

It is about utter repentance

The finger is willing

For the most part

The finger is obedient

Enthusiastic about true unity

For the finger has forgiven

The mouth that bit her.

What's Love?

Love is incredibly humble

Love is amazingly simple

Love is unbelievably modest

Love is remarkably gentle

Love is astonishingly peaceful

Love is astoundingly forgiving

Love is marvelously cool

Love is startlingly lovely

Love is exceptionally meek

Love is marvelously straightforward

Love is implausibly uncomplicated

Love is extraordinarily easy

Love is superbly satisfying

Love is spectacularly rewarding

Love is splendidly pleasing

Love is resplendently fulfilling.

Dignity

Fight back with prayer to God

Fight back with praise to God

Fight back with God's knowledge

Fight back with God's wisdom

Never blow back at the evil wind by yourself

Maximize your meekness incessantly

Focus on the expected good end

As the omnipotent Commander leads

To the honor of His grace

To the excellent height of His ways

Down we kneel as we raise holy hands

Praise we sing as we play saintly bands.

It's Time Y'all

Let's come together

And fight the enemies of progress

For I'm certain of the strength

Of Whom I've entrusted my concerns

Let's come together

And win this war hands down

For we're confident of the might

Of Whom we've handed over our issues

Let's come together

And attack these things vehemently

For I'm convinced of the valor

Of Whom I've handed over these matters

Let's come together

And praise Him in advance

For I'm overly-exceedingly definite

That He'll victoriously victorize them all

God's Encouragement

I know You hear me every time

Sometimes I fancy You'll respond

On my own timetable, of course

But because you're All Knowing

For Your time I'll wait for, Sir

I'm sure that You receive all my praises

Sometime I wonder if they are enough

Regardless of how inadequate that I assume

Or how insufficient that I feel at times

You inhabit in all sincere praises of saints

I'm certain of these roles

Because I rely on Your leadership

Please stand by me, cover me, and hold me

All through these imperative assignments

Please direct me, motivate me, and encourage me.

Genuine Factors

They fell before,

They fell alone.

They resisted falling,

So they arose together.

The fall was easy,

None amongst them anticipated

Even though they had talents,

Selfishness and egotism pushed them down.

They arose though

Talent alone was insufficient.

Two factors in a plan sufficed:

God and genuine unity, so they rose.

I Know Love

Even with delicious baked beans,

Love is superior to BBQ ribs

Even with large worldly connections,

Love is bigger than titles.

Even with lemonized iced water,

Love is superior to pepper soup.

Even with yummy popcorn,

Love is superior to movies.

Even with a mouth-watering sauce,

Love is larger than a steak.

Even with dry meat on a stick,

Love is better than Spumante fre.

Even with a reason or a motivation,

Love is superior to war.

Even with sugar and cream,

Love is more than coffee.

Even with delectable cheese,

Love is superior to macaroni.

Even with luscious stock fish,

Love is more fantastic than ogbono soup.

Even with delicious pepperoni,

Love is healthier than Pizza.

Even with healthy ingredients,

Love is more wonderful than lasagna.

Even with delicious jelly,

Love is more tremendous than a peanut butter sandwich.

United We're Stronger

He evaluates his strength

He breaks every stick that's alone

Baba, the chimpanzee, roars

Baba, the strong, celebrates victory

Baba gamboled in happiness

And found two other vulnerable sticks

Together he put them and tried to break

"Woo woo woooo," he roared in anger

For the two sticks bent, but refused breakage

Baba hopped in anger around the bush

Suddenly another stick

Putting three together, he tried his power

Katakata katakata in ferociousness

For the three sticks were not bent or broken.

Significant 3:16

3:16, numbers of love and faith

Numbers so significant indeed

To our savior, **God's son**, we salute

A splendid sacrifice and love

3:16, also numbers of a birthday

Birthday so momentous in veracity

To our dear **Godson** we celebrate

A diversity of peace and love

God loves us unimaginably and indescribably

That He sent His only Son to die for our sins,

That any person who believes in Him would be saved

And consequently have everlasting life.

Love Defined

Love has no failure within

So successful in entirety

Great everyday in everyway

Plenteous in all dimensions

It does not jealousize or jeopardize

Love is so successful in entirety

It is gainful to love always

Even when containers are not full

Hate is a fool's tool

That deteriorates the beholder's growth

It is always best to love

For love is plenteous in all aspects.

BOUNCING

You are still bouncing

In spite of those wicked tackles

They could have been worse

But you've got Divine connection

Victory was found

Thus organize your testimonies

And claim your victory

For the moment and for the future

It is a spiritual fencing

Protecting your entire household

Fret no method for you are supernaturally encircled

By the conflagration of the Holy Spirit

It was the enemy's notion yesterday

And not God's thought

They conceptionalized a done awful deal

But, wow, you're still bouncing!

WE GOT POWER

We ain't gonna withhold good

From them to whom it is due

When we got the power to deliver

I tarried when informed and advised to wait on the Lord

And God's mercy and power evidenced vividly

And I was endued with power from on high

To proclaim the power in Jesus' blood with a renewed strength

I know I got power from accepting Christ

You too got power from the blood of Jesus

Hence we got power

Through a light that humiliates darkness

And darkness understands it not at all

I got power and I'm a witness

I got power to love all

I got power to fight injustice

Pull no kaput junk immaterialism on me

For I've got power and have been authorized

To trample over serpents and scorpions

And all the powers of the enemies

I got power and I'm a witness

Of God's might and valor.

Ever Blessed

People have no perfection in them

Humans have shifting stances

Satisfied in their insatiable nature

To quest until there's no more to quest

God as a friend understands you

God as a friend listens all the time

God as a friend stands by you always

God as a friend knows your imperfections

People may not share passions

Or interests at times

They bend when they should be straight

They run when they should stand

You are blessed

You are fully loaded

You have a true friend

You have the Most High God.

GOOD HUSTLIN'

No wonder they correct you all the time

The correctors love you and see you've got potential

Don't give up future presidency for bad hustling

Don't you drop out of school, you future leader

If you're going to hustle; if you going to push; push goodness

Nothing fine or good comes easy

If you give quality time to your studies now

You will reap quality grades and a quality career

So no pain, no gain; no sowing, no reaping

I have met people in good professions

Nice houses, fancy outfits, fine cars

They wanted them; they got them via meaningful efforts

But no bad hustlin', no bad pushin', and no bad jostling'

Rebuff constantly looking over your shoulder

As you hustle for God and goodness

And you will smile back at the supernatural being and the community

And keep fit, and praise God, and celebrate!

God Bless You

My family and I prayed for God's grace

We asked God to help us,

And you, and your family,

And we believed in His might.

We also prayed for His guidance

In all life's endeavors

As well as to protect our schools, our homes,

Our churches, and our businesses.

We prayed for you with love

We asked God to watch over you,

In addition to myself, and my family

And your family,

And we believed.

We asked Almighty to bless you in quantum

In every way and everyday

Along with your people, along with our community,

And we believed in His grace.

About the Author

Dr. Udo F. Ufomadu, an award winning author, is a member of the Selma City School Board of Education, Board Member of T.O.P. Education Academy, Board Member of S.C.M., works for the State of Alabama, is an advisor/consultant, a publisher, a Christian songwriter, and a member of Tabernacle of Praise church. He and his wife, Rita, are raising four children--Evelyn, Joy, Ezekiel, and Godson.

To order additional copies call 334.418.4906, 334.418.0088 or

Visit: www.UfomaduConsulting.com, BarnesandNoble.com, Amazon.com,

and other online bookstores

Notes

Notes

Notes

Notes

Notes

Notes

Notes

Notes

www.ingramcontent.com/pod-product-compliance
Lightning Source LLC
Chambersburg PA
CBHW080605010526
44109CB00052B/2354